ART, PASSION, POETRY

by

Barbara Sher Tinsley

Strategic Book Publishing and Rights Co.

Strategic Book Publishing and Rights Co.
USA I Singapore

For information about special discounts for bulk purchases, please contact Strategic Book Publishing and Rights Co. Special Sales, at bookorder@sbpra.net.

ISBN: 978-1-63135-929-3

Book Design: Suzanne Kelly

This poetry collection is dedicated
To my beloved husband, Prof. W.E. Tinsley,
Dearest companion, critic and most faithful audience.

CONTENTS

PREFACE

"As in art," said Horace, "so in poetry."
And he was quite right, too.
Painting does indeed reveal
What poetry makes one feel is true.
All he omitted–love, and passion,
In Roman times was not the fashion.
But art, poetry and love together,
Empowers every fine endeavor.
So, Dear Reader, you will note, I placed
Passion in this boat in which you now set sail,
For love unites both art and verse, improves the two–
Does not make worse whatever may prevail.

1. ART

Art can be a kind of madness–
taking us over, making us its own.
Letting us imagine happy what causes
many others to leave us quite alone.
That which we conceive done beautifully
alienates friends who, dutifully, say when
we present it to them, finished–
"Are you sure you've not the essence
of the thing diminished?"
He who proclaims himself an artist
might better, as Houdini did,
learn the great art of escape.
And isn't that what every artist does?
Escaping what is most drear to us
to find a private beauty?

2. LOVE'S MAGIC

Love, I'm told, is close to magic,
Cannot be explained, they say.
Does not come to one and all,
And has a tendency to stray.
Cannot help at times prove tragic,
Nor prepares one for a fall.

Passion uncontrolled has sway.
Leitmotif of novels, movies and the stage,
Embraces the unloved in its penumbra, unannounced yet
    tender, sage.
Magic love, 'tis stated, openly affects the sated;
But tragic love, its alter ego, goes on tiptoe. Incognito.

3. HUMMINGBIRD WINGS

A hummingbird whose wings whirred neigh
Recalled my summers–long passed by–
When I, a child of six or so
Would run through fields where flowers grow.
Where flowers grew my true love lies…
And I, now agèd, hear his words
When whir the songs of hummingbirds.

4. CONTINUED PASSION

Had I the passion or the clout
to turn heart, brain inside out
and lave them in the gentle rain
that flows to rivers where swim trout–
I think I could unite with stars and
shine like glow-worms in glass jars;
As when we children held aloft
our own; caught in gardens and
on loan from Mother Nature.

Who was she, anyway? Why as we
grew older did we let our hearts
grow colder and instead of bolder unions
with our brains, restrain the acts of love,
thoughts of imagination in the heart;
accompaniment of both to rivers and the
sea; let a cruel step-mother–unnatural–
dictate what could and could not be;
what could not, should not, set us free?

To say what heart and brain conjoined
might yet do? Who gave *her* sway?
Not me. Not you. Then, let us fill our jars
again with light. And run through gardens
at the fall of night; and let us be as we
were at ten, or two times ten and three.
Let us feel again that rush of potency and joy
that made us then, each girl and boy
light-hearted, passionate, free. Who, anyway, *was* she?

5. ARS POETICA

A poem well written bonds the heart–
–a vagabond–with the universe–
and should sustain the lonely soul,
the one who cannot travel free,
yet needs to dream, needs to see–
longs to do what poems can,
reach out freely, self-sustained,
yet anchored to eternity.

A poem written well's a work of
healing, not of vain belief–
relieving sufferers from silence;
beauty's shade, affirming life–
a signature to what was once unsaid;
music passing through the skin, sonata,
rhyme of spirit, daffodils and thyme.

A poem is a lighthouse on the shore
beckoning to one who'd reckoned
on no more direction, safe harbor, joy;
a fare-thee-well in well being; an *envoi*.

Barbara Sher Tinsley

6. WATERCOLOR PAINTING FOR BEGINNERS

I.

I've been painting. A lighthouse, red and white;
four other buildings on the same lateral rocky site
beneath a sky of lavender and blue, orange, aqua, white–
the same multi-colored strokes repeated
in a purple, aqua red and orange sea.
Some might find these mingled hues quite odd,
But colors, lighthouses, rocky promontories,
and little cottages are so Cape Cod.

II.

Having purchased for two bucks, less than passage to *La Suisse,*
I brought home a book of Swiss photos–*exquises*–
And set out just my blue paints-cobalt, cerulean, pthalo,
     ultra-marine–
to paint a splendid mountain range, a stunning mountain scene.
I copied what I saw; I did my best, but there were so many peaks
I soon felt very pressed. Pressed for lack of talent. Pressed for time.
I took a bold black-laden brush and slashed at every sharp incline
until I had completed miles of jagged Swiss terrain.
I did it for economy of time, not monetary gain.

6

III.

Lets go to Martha's Vineyard. All the best folk do.
And there we'll search out an old mill, with waterfall of blue.
The mill was built of mottled stone, each one once filled this field,
Can I, a newly minted artist make this paper, these tints,
this ample clutch of brushes yield an ancient mill?
I spent three days, not steadily, but readily, giving it my all,
exerting every ounce of my artistic will to make this water fall
like water falls in each New England watercourse. And did I?
For the answer to that question I must check *your* source.

IV.

And so to a small lighthouse, one in blue and white,
It sits above the sea, and shines its light on fog,
against a royal blue sky, for it is night, when sailors
seek out what they most need after grog-a sign that
they will reach home port and soon. Tonight, should
disaster befall its lighthouse–master, there's a moon.
Sailors rarely come to grief
When lighted past a moonlit reef.

7. TRIP

Most foreign lands are those
My fingers travel, tracing your
Forehead down to your nose.
Kissing with finger tips your lips
Down your hairy chest and
Belly to your still flaccid etcetera.

There, lingering, my fingers
wondering, reach out to hold
you in my palms. Two work better.
Folding, holding, feeling that
inevitable rise, I glance upward
at your eyes, at your desire.

Much more clearly seen then
when we raised ourselves–
you left, me right–
Onto heretofore impersonal
white sheets and set out to explore
such lovely unknown parts.

What who we climbed and twisted
now alone or two apart entwined have
with limbs that listed down trails
led to the highest peaks.
No cartographer could have missed
the longitude of our exploration.

Of our mounting to
That elevated edge where all
Revealed is revealing–
Before falling into place.
No wonder more wondrous
Than your so refined, lined face.

8. ROUNDING THE EDGES

Is any pleasure of which a writer may avail herself
greater than the steady, oft repeated editing of little
incongruities and sharp edges in her poetry or text?
So like the steady polishing over time of rounded stones
and boulders, even pebbles, by water rushing over them
in brooks where incongruities will not be seen or felt or
noted as they will be in her books.

9. HOPE

If hope were something one could see, some
opaque, concrete entity, then having once
entered in, it would be recognized again,
and like an old, familiar friend, invited thence
to share a while a residence inside the soul.
Alas! Since iridescent and invisible, though invited
in so graciously, it may behave mendaciously,
and make one miserable. The fault is not to evanescence
bound. Hope plays, often without sound, a secondary
role; pain is embedded in a lonely soul.

10. DONNE DEAL

I've one regret about John Donne–that he was only one.
I'd lief rather he were twain; 'twould give me half the pain.
If there were three John Donnes then we'd make four poets in
the glass–that I could see. Of course, one of those would be me.
Even four of such a wit as Donne would not
be more than adequate. So why not four Donnes–
without me? Four could happily–with so much wit
and gravity–thought by some depravity–
handle man's inconstancy–or woman's, rather–
For I gather, he may even had those inconstant
women kissed. And as for those he deemed unjust–
John Donne had no less lust.

Pity his conversion from Rome to Church of England meant
priestly employment. Every day subsequent was
Lent. That caused John to give up, you see, what I trow
his greatest gift to poetry: rhyme with divine irony.
Little rhyme or irony in sermons. Those who liked to hear
John give them, dressed in ermines. Donne's ancestor was
Thomas More, of martyr's status, so did what royalty expected,
fast, with no hiatus. The church job he accepted doomed
eroticism, wit.
Friends of Donne, and maybe Donne, prayed to get much out
    of it.
If not a poet's titillation, then perhaps, his soul's salvation.
When his church's bells did peal, Donne quietly intoned
"Donne deal."

11. MAN'S CONSTANCY (AFTER JOHN DONNE'S "WOMAN'S CONSTANCY")

Now you've made love to me one whole night,
Tomorrow leaving will you say, hey, that was kind of all right?
Will you transfer your promise to some other one?
      Or just declare that it's been fun,
But what the hell, we're not the couple others aim to mime
And that–whenever–we'd be sure to leave behind what we
in the throes of a good screw swore true, others keeping faith
be more apt to do? Or, since marriage, love and death are
dicey propositions, it's not likely either one of us could
stick to what we said we would, not longer than a day.
      Or, just 'til bedtime, say.
For having sworn to change and so changeable, you
Can just easily ditch what you just swore was true.
Egocentric lunatic, among these snares I could
      Dispute, and cream you, and I would,
      Though that I will refrain to do,
For by tomorrow, I, no doubt, shall behave like you.

12. BUT CAN YOU TEACH IT?

Is poetry even teachable?
Is some stranger's head and heart,
sense and sensitivity even reachable?
One thing of which I'm almost sure–
and that's not unimpeachable–
is when you feel yourself a ship whose
sails are billowy and pillowy, *you're*
setting sail for poetry and unbeachable.
Is poetry ever learnable?
It's well known much attempted
was by its authors burnable.
Perhaps their would-be subject wasn't
quite discernible. The poet took a turn
that was not turnable.
In which case he must churn up
something churnable. And yet, it must be said:
Poetry is more than what will butter bread.

13. THE SOUL AND BEAUTY

Does art speak frankly to the soul?
Does soul transform the arts?
Does beauty enter by our fleshly parts,
direct itself to minds? to hearts?

What must a soul's aesthetic be?
That which lasts eternally?
For art and beauty leave a stamp.
Souls drift down every ramp still pure.

Perhaps the soul consigns the beautiful
to hearts and minds because it knows
a truth that artists, poets, painters never chose–
confines itself to what cannot be seen.

Consigns all art to what it deems
the evanescent realm of dreams,
from which the spirit as the soul have
set themselves another goal entirely.

14. PERFECTION

Say then that what we seek and what we find
are never what we have in mind when first we start–
O my dear! Say, too, it's clear that what we arrive at in the end
is more than any blend of happiness that was conceived
before we met, before we dared believe.

Tell no one in your most expansive mood the nature
of our perfect good, and if you could tell, don't.
For no perfection lasts when shared, except with one
whose soul is bared to yours. Let this perfection swath itself
in silk; and then let's shut it off from those not of our ilk.

15. HOW IT IS WITH POEMS

A poem is and is not. Was once
but can no longer be.
Words hint at vanished thought,
at vanished intimacy.
Music minus sound, past healing.
Patterned phonemes on a page
point to phantom pain, depression,
loss, despair or rage.
A poet writing out his heart is so untidy.
Words not articulated; wrong conclusions
dribble off the page. Reflect illusions.

A poem was, but is no longer useful.
Feelings, memories, old scores, reflections–
like things stored in attics are but collections
of life's artifacts. Emotional debris.
A poet's song is something we no longer hear
but only see. A gown, a cloak, unworn
by no one whom we know; by neither you nor me.
A poem was for the poet doubtless rare.
Meaningful and substantive. Now, simply there.

16. GARDENS

Gardens are private places we carefully generate,
so that they may one day regenerate their gardener,
one who gave them care more tender than most lovers could.
For lovers are a feckless lot, and do not take to any plot
as well, as long, as fetchingly as gardens.
Should the gardener find the lone exception, a love without
deception, plant him in your heart where he may grow as
tulips, daffodils and pansies in a row. Lavish on him tenderness.
Toss him each day a kiss. He'll need no further propping up,
as do your morning glory vines. Together you will quench
your thirst for one another on love's sweetest wines.
Lovers must not shun the labor gardeners spend.
For lazy lovers bring to bear in love's own garden naught.
To make that garden a true sheltering bower,
lovers must tend love like gardeners a flower.

17. ETERNAL COMPANY

Long after I have ceased to be
I think that this is true–
I shall not find myself alone,
because I'll think of you.
I'll think of you as once you were
when we first met in June;
I'll think of you with laughing eyes
beneath a golden moon.
With laughing lips and thoughtful gaze
you read my heart full well,
Long after I have ceased to be–
I shall not find myself alone,
For you'll be with me still,
as when you were my own first love,
My sweet, my so romantic Bill.

Barbara Sher Tinsley

18. MY BOOK CLUB, MY DAUGHTER

I thought I had a grasp on lucid prose,
And had arranged for three long years to write
a novel that my book club might one day read.
And though I would attempt to interweave
her story and our family's too, and show
how she affected us, I hoped by doing so
not to diminish any life of hers–
or ours–but to inspire me with hope
that love, and strength of will and sorrow are
the elements of all humanity.

The trick, of course, was keeping cancer–hers–
apart from what we talked about in books;
It lent surcease just temporarily
to dismal grief: watching my belovèd Yve–
though alienated from the family nest–
contriving her escape from certain death.
My daughter's courage, not the books,
engraved upon my heart a certain joy–
For though great novels can distract and teach,
lessons lie embedded there we cannot reach.

19. POETRY'S STAIRCASE

A poem is a circling stair that
leads the spirit circling there, then
launches it where, taking flight, it bears
the heart into the night;
and ever circling up beyond
reminds the soul of what it's fond.
A poem can do things, you see
without the ambiguity of prose;
For prose can only fill the mind–
which leaves the spirit far behind
and does not launch the soul to flight
but leaves it waiting out the night.
A poem is a gift of light,
while prose makes passable the night.
A poem changes how we dream,
while prose explains why things may seem.

20. WHAT IS POETIC SPEECH?

Poetry is language beating in the heart.
Some say verse. But verse is a poor explanation.
For what is that but justification for distorted speech?
Poets are not verbal contortionists, nor exist to entertain.
They are guides to memory and meaning, pointing to
reflections blanched by sunshine, drenched by rain.

Walk beside a poet. One will penetrate a kind of wall–
a certain emotional impasse not otherwise pierced at all.
Poetic utterance creates a breech between what is and
is not conveyed by ordinary speech; builds a bridge for each.
And so inspires introspection; ethical reflection upon
what can most definitively be grasped by a poet's reach.

Poetry plants flowers in the mind where they bloom forever.
Metric language resounds in every fiber of the soul's tympanum,
to die out never. Poetic speech is how a poet makes each hearer
whole, creates new vistas measured by extension, intension,
invention; a new scale of immensity, intensity and awareness.
Poetry is thereness.

21. PASSION'S FOOLS: IN HONOR OF W. B. YEATS

We are all passion's fools.
And too many are there who
too conveniently forget it.
We are all fashion's tools,
and so we should admit it.

For every brave and honest sinner,
some old cheat claims he's a beginner.
Who quickly denigrates his worth
surely benefits this earth.
Of candid folk there is a dearth.

Why have I opened up these gates?
The reason? I just put down Yeats–
Of course no one can put him down.
He wasn't any sort of clown to be put down.
No, take him up for a full crown.

A crown would, I think, have suited him.
His poetry harks back to all men crowned
with vim and lust, and so it's only just
that at a ripe age he did vow that women still
did please him then. Again, again and yet again.

And if a man like Yeats admits, that the old urging
were not for purging, a modern poet can be
expected to echo him, for he's respected.
And if that poet's another gender, I think Yeats
would at her gates be just that much more tender.

22. POETRY AND POETS

Who knows the poetry of soul? remembers a long-ended goal
of that ultimate poetic place that once, like a half-grown foal,
jumped the pasture gate and trotted away; relieved of any
and all constraint?

Poetic spirit, muse of my heart, follow that foal and just once
set my heart to trotting, too. For trotting to a canter turns
and then galloping, discerns a landscape of more brilliant hues.
Make it happen, Muse!

Who knows the poet trapped inside a framework, caught inside
a cage of glass with feelings dry, and rage so wry that lets no
inspiration nigh? Who sees him thus and regrets not the poet's
scourge of being ever on the verge of divine music?

If so, let's weep. For poets and poetry keep us from that final
sleep that ends all joy. Come, let us rejoice that having heard a
poet's voice we may with grace and sharing avoid the poet's
threnody: trilling his melody of love and caring.

23. BIRD FLIGHT

Watching bird flight by the ocean shore,
a poet asks: are there words that
do as adequately soar?

24. BRIDGES

A bridge most simply fills a void, a space,
and lets you get from place to place.
You cross it leaving parts behind that you
may or may not ever find. A lover, garden,
books and such. Crossing bridges can cost much,
and having done, you're out of touch.
Every crossing takes its toll on what
you thought would be your goal.
Though you crossed it over Roman arches,
framed by cypress trees or larches;
or drove across a steel suspension,
you'll not escape the apprehension that
doth fundamentally derive from being
where you hope to thrive.
Transitions inevitably involve
a passage you alone resolve.
Oft a bridge extends an invitation
to your whole life's re-creation.

25. GOETHE'S THEORY—TURNER'S STORM

Goethe theorized that certain colors–
blue, blue-greens and purple had a
minus quality that caused a viewer to be
anxious, restless, susceptible–
To what exactly? Goethe did not mention
any circumstance or thing perceptible.

But Joseph William Mallard Turner took
him at his word, and "*In the Evening of the Deluge,*"
though Goethe's theory smacked of the absurd,
transformed his principles into a most anxiety
producing scene–a central void, vortex of white
inscribed, encircled by a sky of blue and green.

While underneath a heath of yellow, green and
purplish brown, without a tree, a stone,
a cottage, road or town lay tumbled, jumbled
in a royal welter. Oh, Turner, couldn't you
have given us to withstand this storm some
hint of minimal, if symbolic shelter?

Painters, like poets, I believe, would do their best
to draw a curtain over theories of Romantics who,
like themselves, would leave us *angstlich* or uncertain.

26. ON "A SONG" BY W. B. YEATS

Yeats wrote, *"O who could have foretold*
that the heart grows old?"
when his body showed its age?
He wrote that bold upon the page.
Bold it was, but was it sage?

He wrote, *"I have not lost desire,"*
but thought his heart had no more fire;
And that a woman could not get
From words what "satisfied" her yet.

He said he was *"no longer faint"*
when at *"her side;"* one blushes at such pointless pride.
William Butler got it wrong; his fire
was just what lit his *"Song."*

Youth, he wrote, he couldn't prolong by using *"dumb-bells"*
And a 'foil.'" Those weren't what made his old heart boil.
As long as he'd not lost desire,
he could have kindled her a fire.

27. DOUBTING THE MUSE

Every writer and of course all poets doubt their muse.
The act of composition is not all about composing.
Inadequacy, lack of talent, talented competitors
make writing not an act of steady opening but quite
often one of indeterminate and frequent closing.

Closing as a tulip's petals do at night, before the sun
upon the morrow's kissed them open, a kiss that often
makes them start with that self-doubt that makes the
loveliest of tulips in the night to pine, console themselves
with what seems premature floral decline.

We novelists and poets woo our muse, but not with so much
confidence we feel our suit is won. We suspect we've but just
begun. Whatever triumphs that were ours as writers, we're
unwisely authorized to trumpet. Who better than a jilted
lover or a slighted writer has reason to believe their Muse a
strumpet?

But even doubting, since as authors doubt we must, we reap
benefits in doubt's pursuit. Those who publish thick tomes
oft win distinction, bank much loot. But ask a tyro from whom
the world's not heard, and he'll say it's doubt that draws him on
from word to yet unpublished word.

28. MANDOLIN

A lobe of fitted wood, black like a sweet peach rotting,
and a face tinted to aging honey.
Twelve pegs on a neck bent back–
Uncontemporary attack on progressive jazz.
Mandolin. Scent of half-remembered time.
Of song under lilac.

29. RAINBOWS

Rainbows would not exist but for refraction.
Their colors are not even mist, and yet of all the
sensual things that I have known that do exist–
and quite a few of those I've kissed–
Rainbows, though short-lived, and really never lived at all–
hold out for me the most attraction.

30. NUDE PORTRAITURE

Is it rude to draw a nude?
So many have been painted.
And here's a thought–
all that was wrought
by some other nude's been painted.
For under an artist's clothes,
you must suppose, there lies
another one. Not nude for fun.
Men have painted mostly women
without clothing, not unclothèd men.
We female artists should respond
by painting the male nude so then
the other sex could better see
how when unclothed nudes weren't free
to hide the flaws most all possessed
of too much flab, too little chest;
of mottled skin, not well muscled,
of feeling chilly, silly, hustled.
I think if women drew men nude
most models would be apt to brood
as women do when private tissue
appears small, deflated, drapey.
Men wouldn't be elated if their tissue were
the issue; and just as flaccid, just as crepey.

31. SIMILES OF THE POETIC SELF

I am as if I lived in beams of shade,
in gleams that reaching deep inside a glade
provide at once my shelter and my stage.
I am a soul impressionable–filled to the
brim with happiness, delirium and rage.

Were I an e. e. cummings, I'd doubtless
be more sprightly. Walt Whitman–
speak profoundly, and more lightly.
Robert Frost, more naturally and fresh.
Emily Dickinson? Keep thoughts inside a
Reticule of lacey and impenetrable mesh.

32. PAINTING LIFE

We start our lives a wash. No lines; no color, wet. Nothing sure
except–perhaps–our genitals, heredity.
Any details, outline, shadowing, highlights, strong lines, mist,
mystery, must be added slowly, delicately traced by DNA; later
colored carefully. Depression, Payne's grey and blue; isolation–
burnt umber, ivory black; jealousy, yellow ochre mixed with
viridian; love–alizarin crimson splashed with violet; use with
discretion if you try it.

Our personality and appearance can clash garishly with our
surroundings, invariably not be of our making. Painting life is
not living it. Limned by circumstance, filled in by an artist of
moderate skill, we cannot even if we will, bring this picture off
to please all viewers in the gallery. Through which we, richly
framed, or loosely rolled, go strolling by bored museum guards.
This is the Gallery of Life. Once you pass the rotunda,
you may pose for pictures, there between the ficus and the fern.

33. MODERN LOVERS SCRIPTED

Nothing under great Apollo's sun has
not been said already. Would any
modern couple talk if conversation were
first constrained to be direct, correct,
straightforward and steady?
Forward enough so if they had the stuff
they could at once proceed to passions heady?
That is, to sex unscripted, unencrypted, following
speech, which now *is* scripted, transcribed–
but seemingly beyond the modern couple's reach?
Had they some romantic rhetoric, rather than
four letter words preferred–where would a modern pair
repair to find the mold for such rhetorical exchange?
The range today is foreplay electronic. No one attempts
the merely phonic. To wit, and wit is shorter in supply,
on what have modern lovers to rely? Nothing platonic.
So much today is foreordained by social media:
Google, Facebook, Twitter, Wickipedia.
Limiting messages to the liminal, minimal, subliminal.
Programmed and impersonal rhetoric of proposal.
Stilted. Pathetic. Synthetic. At everyone's disposal.
Tweets of forty syllables, a password, "ugly name"
or hashtags are now as far as any two can see, the
necessary forms of intimacy that need be intimated.
A wedding scene. A bedding–seen of course with
intercourse (non verbal), but in virtual reality on every
possible–and much these days is possible–type of
electronic screen. There, several thousand of their closest
inarticulate dear "Friends" can hardly wait 'til they attend–
of course–this modern couple's equally scripted, un-

encrypted, electronic, well articulated divorce. Fine.
But that must wait until next year, perforce.
Their wedding, is of course, as yet unpaid for.

34. POETS ON PEOPLE

Poetry for people's made, not people for poetry.
Poetry for people's made and will not vanish in the shade of a
Poet's remorse. Of course, most fear to look their mentors–
people–in the eyes, press them to their breasts, even those
whose lives they would feign enter.

While gods and goddesses, nymphs, naiads and knights
are easy to flesh out, people remain mysterious
in the round and often deleterious when found. And so,
poets arrange to find them most often when they're–
people, not poets–in a coffin.

W. H. Auden wrote on Walter Butler Yeats, it's true,
and on some writer–a real blighter–named Nixon, too.
"Chaplinesque's" the title of a poem by Hart Crane–
But you'll seek your whole life long before discovering
what any of these men were hiding; knew of pain.

Collectivities? There's Alan Tate's *"Ode to the Confederate dead."*
It must be said that not one of those dead was named. Might
as well poeticize on toads or loads of rancid grain stacked
up in the rain. The Yankees may have killed them all, with
equanimity,
but Tate kept them beneath a pall of anonymity.

Shall we consider Archibald Macleish's *"You, Andrew Marvell?"*
Pardon me, but what the hell can one tell of Andrew here?
The poem's a mere title–and it's about exotic places.
No Andrew Marvell there. Who knows if Andrew liked
those places? Macleish had not one marvelous word to spare.

Barbara Sher Tinsley

Conrad Aiken had a great one on Verlaine and Rimbaud.
Both poets argued about iambs, spondees. Finally,
like Shakespeare and so many others–like us all–they fell to rot.
So what of Verlaine's character or Rimbaud's sentiments
have we got? Not a whole hell of a lot.

John Crowe Ransom wrote on Judith of Bethulia,
a Hebrew belle whom some thought would go to hell.
She did her duty naked, clothed. Played on lyres that she
loathed. Warmed her feet at some lover's fire. Handsome if
Ransom
Had attributed to Judith–or any other soul–a bit of human
desire.

35. MEMORY

Memory's a lightsome thing–holding on
by thinnest string of cells within the cranium to
thoughts of birth, of death, the scent of a geranium.
Teased by time, revived by chance–
perfume, lemons, iris, daffodils and wine–
candles glowing in a mind we
thought had ceased to pay attention.
Memory is reality's re-invention.

36. RONDEL FOR WRITERS

Words once penned come back to haunt a writer.
What any author writes exceeds his grasp forever.
Poems, memoirs, novels once finished ever
Like mushrooms after rain the world make brighter.
His dreams, fears, fantasies pull his nerves e'er tighter,
For having been inscribed, though not in his eyes clever,
Words once penned come back to haunt a writer,
What any author writes exceeds his grasp forever.
Who, on writing painfully, does not feel himself a fighter?
Besting odds, chain barriers his sword alone could sever.
No matter though how costly or successful his endeavor,
Words once penned come back to haunt a writer.

37. SATIETY AND LONGING

There should be a balance betwixt longing and satiety.
It seems propriety could not make do with less–
This has a history most ancient–
owing not to parsimony but mistrust of happiness.
I believe there is a wisdom to living with restraint,
And self indulgence has become a modern curse.
But surely wise men differentiate between consuming
reasonably and that which simply overloads one's plate.
Can one be too loyal to one's lover? have too much
passion once beneath the cover? Can one reach satiety
in art, in charity, in caring for each other? Longing for the
worthiest of treasures, must we put a maximum on pleasures?
Satiety is not the other side of longing–all appetites can
never equal be. What satisfies the one may cloy another,
and every pair of eyes sees differently. No surfeit of seeing
corrupts our view; longing may provide our soul sight too.

38. RESTLESS

Restless. *Rastloss. Agité.* There is a constant wind today.
I cannot think. I cannot dream. I'm not the writer that I seem.
Or maybe wind, dust, agitation act as solvents to creation.
I might say creativity. If I didn't more's the pity. Poets
undone by weather, should throw it over altogether.

Restless. *Irrequieto, sollicitus*, upset. How many kinds of
disquietude are there anyway to get? *En Espanol agitata?*
Two years of high school Spanish? *Nada.*
The point is when I'm most in need of inspiration all
distraction keeps my brain from recourse to poetic action.

Quite the opposite of poetry occurs when one is restless;
intellectually chained unto the drear noetic, one says
adieu to the poetic. Now blow unslaked, unswept, misshapen
banks of memories, formed by flakes like snow upon my walk.
Too restless to engage as I so long to do in sweet poetic talk.

39. PERMANENCE

What things tell me, shall abide?
Moon, stars, sun, tide.
And name the ones that shall resound–thunder, birdsong,
waves that pound against the pilings of the docks; crickets of a
summer night, babies wailing, chiming clocks.

And what will be those that flee?
Youth and beauty principally. Next, memories of times that
passed. Children grown,
friends that passed. Events and faces blended, blurred.
The poignancy of loving lovers long interred.

40. COMMANDMENT #2

Oceans I have never seen, beaches never wandered–
Rock impearled, waves unfurled, not one sand grain squandered.
God the Artist–Creator God, maker of all beauty
Let us experience critically your artwork; enjoin it as our duty.
For all designs for us begun have now been vandalized, each one.

The loveliness that You, O Artist from on high made,
But forbade us represent–O God, the artist,
in the name of creativity, relent. Equip us with a palette like
Your own, that makes war and greed and ugliness for profit's
sake an isolated beach off limits; unpainted, not posed; a crone.

Let us repent abominations; shame we create daily in Your name.
You did say, did You not, "Vengeance is mine alone?"
Great Artist, Creative spirit, deity of art, paint out war and
nationalism; efface the drone. Let us make beauty, diplomacy,
peace, brotherhood and sisterhood our own.

41. CONFESSION OF A SINFUL SEEKER AFTER FAME

One goes, if Catholic, to confession to admit one's deepest sins. The worthiest of blame. I'm no Catholic, but confess my worst is fame. Not its possession. I clarify in my confession that I've none of which to boast. It's just the wish for it I'm prone to commit most. After what penance, pray, may I receive the Host?

I do not wish for riches, beauty. I am willing to pursue my current duty, which is writing every day my memoir; or my novel. My new passion–poetry–consumes a loathsome passion to be taken for a Poet–though–one lamentably out of fashion. I know I am to blame.
I rhyme. *Culpa mea.* Damnable, old fashioned shame.

I do avow that I'm enthralled by meter. Unlike St. Peter who denied Christ thrice without. And to expel all doubt, I'd say the rosary, but only in the form of poesy, thus adding to my sins. To be transparent with my Parent up above, I do profess my love of lyricism, meter, comprehensibility. For these, I take full responsibility.

"Forgive me Father, for I know I've sinned." These stanzas that I've drawn from out my mental well are apt, I know, to send my soul to Hell. But poets are transvestites of the heart; they beat in no one form and are peculiarly upstart; claiming more depth than they are worth. But hasn't that been true of so much creativity on this earth?

42. RAIN, DROUGHT, POETRY

I remember when it rained–before the drought came
And lowered reservoirs of memory until the level
Dropped too low to recreate poetry about our past.
I remember when it rained life was caressed by
gentleness; reproved by rain's ferocity.
We lived in Texas, Michigan, Missouri, Wisconsin.
Oh, I remember how it rained in Madison.
I ran down Bascom Hill, soaking to my skin,
and there you were, admiring how I looked
so wet in my home-made shirt and shorts. Nineteen.

Now the drought has gripped sweet California.
We scan each day the blue bright sky where sunshine
turned my spigot dry against poetry; affording me a mere
sporadic drip. My reservoir of metric verse has dropped
below the level of its once so fluid flow.
The drought has had its way with me and poetry.
Not that the garden suffers. I water it each day and
in this way defy the lack of rain that keeps my spirit dry.
Denying a pervasive doubt that when or if the rain
returns, I won't remember inundation.

I may find that rain has not washed poems
in again; but like the drought, has cleared them out.
And life goes on. I–dependent on this California sky
beneath which I have loved and lived and written
history, memoirs, novels from a reservoir of life–
Might I not wonder if to a large degree,
it has been mere weather that produced in me
such creativity? Such Love? For plainly, all that
has rained down on me–and I remember rain–
came only from above. I remember rain, and Love.

43. NO "EMPTY DOCUMENTS" EXISTED THEN

Once poets wandered out to fields, or sat by streams
recording dreams of love and loss; where, if they chose,
they'd toss a crumpled thought they'd spoiled, into the brook
as one might carelessly clip and toss a less than perfect rose.
That such times would soon return I never would suppose.

They'd start out early. Wrap their noonday provender in a
kerchief, leave at seven; under skies then getting
pearly in Apollo's heaven. Poetry was their end of days–
and inspiration; indolence and reverie their leaven.
They wrote, returning when the sun was just then setting.

Inspiration's all they had with which to raise on paper a
    touching verse
of happiness or consolation to overcome suffering and pain;
for rhyme was magical; and hence, if not the only one, the most
effective medicine that poets–doctors of the soul–could to the
suffering self dispense.

Words are not magical today. We spew them out as if to say,
Have done with beauty, meaning, meter, rhyme –invented for
another time, when it was the fashion to ponder what constituted
empathy, what passion. Now we have the cure they sought.
Instant messaging of naught.

44. CHANGE OF SEASON

The winds are blowing as winds will,
and prairie grasses bend and sway.
The dust is tossed up from the hill
and from the marsh, a whip–poor–will
sings and repeats his roundelay.

The summer, ending, leaves behind
its soft bouquets of love. I find
them dried and faded, yet,
I save them in their vases still.
Awaiting fresh blooms from spring's hill.

O summer! Fading as you must,
shall I reproach you as unjust?
Or, like the blowing grasses bend,
forgetting thus my summer friend?
You will return, and so shall he, I trust.

45. LOVE OF GRAY EYES

If gazing into eyes so gray
could make me love another way,
and loving, make me longer keep
the love that would not ever sleep–
Then I could take each evening gray,
Command it; make it hold its sway forever.
And through your love, and in your eyes remain
unchanged and never give o'er gazing.

Barbara Sher Tinsley

46. LEAPING OFF

In dreams, it seems, we have the power
to spread our arms and fly–
to jump off from the top of roofs
and lay our bodies bye.

So then at death we'll do the same
and from this dour crust leap–
minus body weight or blame
and launch ourselves where none need sleep.

Free from worry, free from flesh
released in every part.
Our spirits shall find perfect rest
from all but love; but art.

47. PASSPORT

A door that can be opened can be closed.
A secret that was hidden be exposed.
Letters but half written be destroyed.
So many passage ways exist to
get us through or to or over what we
might otherwise have missed.

Barbara Sher Tinsley

48. LOVE'S DUTY

What, wondered I was a lover's duty?
The reverence paid the loved one's beauty?
Perhaps the rhythmic beating of two hearts together;
and severance of all former ties–
paired denial of the other's prior tender sighs?

A lover's booty's security of attachment–
sacred sign of love's purity, "as long as we both may live"?
No question asked about how much to give? Love's beauty
is to do whatever love desires. Love's duty
is to light and keep lit love's sacred fires.

But doesn't duty make of love a task?
Should not the lovers one another ask
from time to time, "My dear, is our love today as
sweet as when we tasted of it just last year?
Is the wine of love as red, the glass as clear?"

For love that is a duty mere may turn out
for good or ill to be a labor onerous
that goes against each other's will, desire, too, and
then love's duty may well be only
to part with kindness saying "Adieu."

49. PASSION'S FIELD

Come, take my hand and run with me,
Through fields of daisies, buttercups,
Where sip the hummingbird, the honey-bee,
There will you like honey be to me.
There will I like butter be to you,
Hearts like hands entwined, we'll on
Each other as do birds, bees, flowers dine.

50. DARKNESS

You told me once you were afraid of the dark.
But dark is blessed. It holds the light at bay
and gives our souls a chance to lay completely
and discreetly down to rest; to set off on a quest
to what is best about our knowing one another.
How could any lovers dare to know each other
wholly, solely in the light? To see with benefit
of mere sight what can be better felt in darkness
of the night and by the body, keenest of senses.
Kindest, too, and of most revelatory recompenses.

And then comes day, and with it, pray what can be
Seen by shape, by hue, by tint of skin and hair that
me, that you, did not already in the night–devoid
of light intuit? Daylight to the world unknowable
belongs; through its glare how should we ever even
dare reveal what we together share in darkness?

51. HOLD ME TIGHT

Hold me, hold me tight. Hold me
for all we're worth–so should this–could this?–
be our last night on earth, departing for the stratosphere
with our mutual smile, we can indeed attest
that we were blessed. It was a love worthwhile.

Barbara Sher Tinsley

52. ALL TOPICS TAKEN

If all topics poets treat were someday to be taken,
I think that I, a poet, too, would not feel shaken.
Love, sorrow, landscape, including flowers, trees
and every kind of bird and beast–I'd still feel at ease.
I should sit down with me alone, seated on the
World's anthologies and laugh, not moan. Because
poetry is, titles set aside, a place where single
souls abide. And every poet, individual, shelters
his own melodious words and thoughts residual.
When all is read and done, 'tis Thou who brought me
rays of sun–and made the darker hours flee–
Bound together, you and me.

53. LOVE IN SOFT LIGHT AND SHADOWS

Shadows falling as we descend, sun dropping off behind.
Shades and brightness, love and lightness
Penetrating heart and mind. O, Love! Please be so
Kind as to enlighten my dimmed view
Of shade and shadows, memories erotic
And kissing you.

What sheltered rest, what dreams made bright
While overhead a forest loomed,
Whose mossy floor revealed a clearing. How it bloomed.
Here let us lie again on mounds midst forest sounds
And recollect a love more clearly limned than ever was
In lamp lit rooms; in light by sunset dimmed.

54. ARISTOTLE'S POETICS

Poetry like art itself, works to imitate nature–
even if Nature, as the Stagirite propounded,
would rather be propounded with what is universal
than what changed; and so omit poetry's sweet rehearsal
of all that we may do: except philosophize on what is true.

Aristotle did allow that poetry's an art persuasive and may
on occasion be invasive and analogize–if wise–on oratory,
morality, politics and learning. That's because all these are art
forms of poetic yearning, which translates as persuasion. Poets
may deform, re-form these arts to suit their own occasion.

But the sage, viewing the declivities of the theater, the rising of
the stage, did warn: that tragedy, another art, must needs be set
apart, and that because its form is not persuasion as is poetry
and other subjects cited; all of which can unite to change the
mind. The poet obeys to be enrollèd with his kind.

That leaves tragedy, the only other poetry that simply is.
Which no art, my dear, may change or make more pretty.
Tragedy's the sole poetic form that can't be altered–except it
move your heart to fear and pity. Poetry observes that dictum
with calm, leaving tragedy the aching soul's universal balm.

55. FANCIFUL MIGRATION

A poet's flights of fancy, unlike the flight of birds
migrates not from place to place
but by the grace of words. Poets in mid passage,
caught up among the clouds, find their way by thinking
thoughts out loud; birds find their way by DNA.

A poet's flight of fancy unlike that of birds
is never pre-determined, but his flight is one of words–
which are a rout–and not a route–
affected oft by pain acute;
or by mere chance; his flight not unlike a dance.

A poet's flight is one of longing, not belonging
to impulse physiological–
His flight of fancy is chancy; not logical,
not ingrained. He lacks a natural call to spread his wings
and yet…a poet's flight requires him to spread out things.

So migratory thoughts send him aloft toward Heaven
and mounting, he sings to pass the time. He calls it rhyme.
Flights poets take do not such long migrations make–
But flights of poets and of birds are flown
with natural blessings for our common sake.

56. POETRY'S LOVER

Nothing in me more dispels
Ennui than writing villanelles,
Nor removes my sadness, say,
Than getting off a triolet.

I have no bees inside my bonnets–
So leave me be, just writing sonnets.
And if you do, then you may fondle
My most brassy, sassy, private–rondel.

For I am not shy nor pristine–Ah!
For you I'd write my best sestina.
Now leave me to my pen and paper.
Ease my labor. Light my taper.

If I cannot cheer us both–
Then brand me a poetic sloth.
What? Everything I've writ, you loathe?
Then find another to unclothe.

For I have stripped myself quite bare,
Writing verse antique and fair.
Then fare thee well. *Adieu. Adieu.*
I'll squander not my muse on you.

Not me, my pen, I'll now lay down;
Do take your purse. I have my crown.
When dressed and veiled in poetry
I'll find a lover who's more true to me.

57. MEMORIES OF LOVE, A SONNET

I think at times how I once sang of love,
Of those sweet days of lustiness and joy,
Wherein each swain reached down from above
To prove how tenderness could move that boy.
But now, reflecting how the years have flown,
How memory has kept alive their flame,
I've thought of all the bounties that I've known,
Yet also how each one was not the same.
No shadows no, nor shades across me pass,
Despite the sand that's running all the while,
Nor any force could make me say "Alas,"
Since images of youth just make me smile.
Such constancy and caring by my mate,
Has more than girlish memories set straight.

58. PLACES

There are places of the memory, places in the mind;
and there are faces from those places that one
ought not leave behind. So in the lock box of my
soul I have them all confined.

There are places we have traveled,
lived in, loved and lost–
Spaces so unique, so valued, they
must be preserved at any cost.

Hearts attach to places as to people loved
and known. I had rather keep my places
than anything I own. But if, dear, we be parted,
I would think of you alone.

59. COMPOSITION EMERGING

Is any painter in control of every streak or line?
Or does she let herself be guided by the whole design?
I know when I, with laden brush in hand
before my easel sit or stand I have in mind
what trembling hand cannot then convey.

But artists do not embrace defeat,
Rather let their minds compete with
each misguided ill conceivèd stroke–
Until persistence has its way, and ten or
twenty strokes repay the one that went awry.

So, too, do I think the artist of the universe,
seeing She had left the sky for worse for
having painted too few stars, daubed in an
another trillion. Until her composition, finished
neatly, overwhelmed the critics so completely.
Not one objected when, during an eclipse,
She made the moon vermillion.

60. HOUSE LIGHT

If I were but a lighthouse
high above the shore
I would light your ship to harbor,
and you'd be grateful. What is more,
you would climb the rock formation,
having roamed about the coast,
and find the eyes, those gleaming orbs
that brought you me as host.

I am, alas, no lighthouse,
nor live beside the shore.
Those lights that gleam
are closed and dream of
delights yet in store.
I do not know a traveler, not one
on land nor sea. Still, I think my cottage lamp
will light your way to me.

61. MAY

Poets once made May their month of choice, and
come what may I speak now in their voice. As you may not in May,
so shall the oysters uneaten make you long for
September–any month which has an "r;" which May has not.
Are you following so far?

The darling "buds" of May might cause some
trouble–depending on her age. But no one can deny her
flowery meads and natural needs that always raise a blush.
Despite the crimes of someone flush as May, to which
Shakespeare was alluding, Hamlet was the one upon them
brooding.

Shakespeare may have in May's sweet bower kissed.
The month of May was all a-flower, designated fresh.
And were he "Lord in May" and were you "April's lady," even
Swinburne would confess to something shady. Remember
Chaucer's "parfit knight" was "fresh as is the month of May."
Antique poets got me started on this month, you say?

Such mania is what makes me as a poet conclude that
there's a deal of good to get in some May wood, would only
that I might. But if I may not than might it be some other site.
"For May wol have no slogardie a nyght. The season priketh
every gentil herte/ And maketh hym out of his slep to sterte."
(Chaucer).

There are other topics poets have spat from out their maw, sir.
Mallory accused the month of being "lusty." Hearts, too, were
lively in the manner of a lover; and Goldsmith gave it all away
–oh, he was hot–referring to the "lap of May that might by
ling'ring winter yet be chilled." And therefore not with child be
filled due to cold? Or what? Is May too chilly to make bold?

I could go on for hours. How sweetly May quaffed April's
showers. How the freshest, purest, fairest was by mayhem,
too, imbued; the first pole dance–a Maypole–Puritans deemed
lewd. Disgusted, they outlawed May's Queen–sweet sixteen–
large chested. Such amplitude dread sensuality suggested.
May anciently provided hope for a year's improved nutrition.
Trees or poles symbolized fruit and fuel; so next winter's
starving could be held at bay by storing up what bees had
fertilized in May. Satiety, not propriety was the reason.

May was spirit, lust, a lucky chance; a romp around a tree.
Ancient and symbolic rites not just for fertility, but for a better
season.

62. EXILED BY POETIC MEANS

What do I know of poetry? Why bother to ask at all? It picks me up without my comprehension; then pushes, rather, hurls me out through corridors tall of bright white light and glass–depositing my trembling frame by tension set aflame outside with consummate condescension–onto a field of yellowish, dry, sterile, yellow, waving, prickly grass, shouting to me in shade, "Go, make something of this!" But of what in all this exile and alone-ness is there to be made?

Outed, I find no kindred soul at all. I'm in a total daze, half hidden by the waist high swells of dry straw grass; looking back, lump throated, I gaze under a dim star with awe and jealousy upon acquaintances with whom, I might have made the dull time in some room or bar pass cordially. If only I had not been rushed so willfully and intentionally–so existentially divided from their happy, laughing mass. That invitation to remain contentedly n'er came to pass.

What I do know of poetry is from the soul;
it parts poets like me from shared posterity and in austerity deprives them of comradery–the common goal. It keeps the poet ever liminal and minimal and, some think, vaguely criminal, while he or she is separated out from common touch and all such as comes to others naturally. Poets endure incomprehension, condescension; enjoy no benefits of easy friendship, love; the healing and appealing kiss of ordinariness.

Barbara Sher Tinsley

63. EDITING A LIFE

I haven't finished writing. Yes, the work needs editing.
Whom might I hire? Any volunteers for work containing
laughter, lust, unjust and copious, unanticipated tears?

I didn't pick all the subjects; some picked me. Notwithstanding,
isn't it authorial to make them a memorial? Even those that slip
my mind? Editors do, I find, shape works of this very kind.

Girl met boy. Shared joy in love, work, children, friends.
Fought. Taught history, philosophy. Made amends. Kids. Life's
dividends. Opposed war with all our heart. Watched our
children grow apart.

Editors like good transitions. They bring forth (Lat., *edere*)
public editions whose dialogue of thoughts and pain, fuse
perfectly so readers might gain insight into others' lives.

For those lacking in it by their own admissions.

68

64. WHAT UNDONE?

And if when all was said
Something there was that
Was not done,
Who could determine, who decide,
That one thing that was set aside?
Who for witness could they find
To testify as to my mind,
When all was done and said?
When all who knew me,
Loved me, laughed and slept
With me; and on that something
missing wept with me–are dead.

65. FOG NEAR SAN FRANCISCO

Elusive, intrusive, the fog billowed from a high diagonal
that lowered almost imperceptibly, where
its amorphous shape perceptibly enveloped us. Slower, grayer,
until each misty moving layer had descended to
just overhead, surrounded us and made unclear our view.

You, feeling its cooling touch, fog fingers on your skin
feared it would close upon us, lock us in its embrace.
But then, ascending higher on the hill beside our winding road
we glimpsed its provenance–the sea–slate brown, silver, agate-
striped chalcedony; anything but blue.

You said the fog intruded on our privacy; then,
blowing down a valley filled with rooftops more
colorful than the sea eluded us entirely. It could
not expunge what it did not recognize. And, searching
for its mate, took off to find it past the Golden Gate.

66. HEALING SPIRIT

What spirit can a grieving heart
invoke to heal it?
Which has the power and the
will to repeal a daughter's passing?
Tell me, and I'll do everything I can
to seal it in my soul.
To serve as a preservative of what
her passing from me stole.

67. A LEARNER'S LEGACY

Were I to tell you all I know
you might think I fell below
a certain standard erudition.
But what I've learned's in poor condition,
neglected now for many years. I don't
recall much that I once knew,
and have no urge now to review.
But I am wise in other modes–
You'd be surprised, but I've learned loads
of things you'd never use, and most
of what I learned refuse. Each one
must carry knowledge lightly;
I have and am not so unsightly.
What I've imbibed from archives hidden,
Is more than you'd imbibe if bidden.
If only I could share these now
that I'm so wise and don't know how.

68. LIGHTHOUSE

A lighthouse white, sun-splashed, a slough–
Water, triangulated blue.
Banks of grasses; no one passes.
Only me and thoughts of you.

A lighthouse in the day is blind.
It cannot leave light trails behind
or throw them far, far out to sea
seeing you, watching me.

If I were built thus on a bluff
I think I'd feel purpose enough
if days were fair, and then, night air
blew you to me, and me, too, there.

69. NEUROHUMANITIES: WHAT IS "SCIENTIFICALLY" BEAUTIFUL AND TRUE

As writers, artists, poets–aestheticians of the old familiar sort–
Impelled by images, subtlety, context, meaning, form,
you have may have overlooked what has become a new norm:
Neurohumanities, electronic measurement of beauty,
the brain's subtlest retort.

Deciding what might be salvaged from the Arts curriculum
is now trending. Measurement of art by Magnetic Resonance
Imaging makes attending to electronic calibrations
of the value of a book, painting, and beauty budget building,
self-serving, and unnerving–an academic duty.

"Hybrid culture"–art plus science may deride
what is and isn't beautiful. Technology only can provide the cash
that will eventually decide what beauty is; what trash.
"New Lit Crit" urges skeptics to agree that beauty
be critiqued scientifically.

The reader of a great book, poetry or prose undergoes an
MRI that will expose if readers read the item properly; were
correctly moved at certain junctures. The worth while-ness of
the work may be disproved; and audience and artists all for
unlovely invention, suffer from the critics' sharpest punctures.

Literature professors are now "proving" what's literary and
moving is as capable of scientific proof as physics or geology.
They're not writing an apology for what doesn't measure
up to snuff. Facebook, Corsera, Google, Amazon–enough.
Digitization is truth; beauty measured by what is and isn't stem
stuff.

74

At least before, the criticism of a novel, a sculpture or a scene well painted was judged by those who were themselves in humanistic studies educated. Criticism was still an art, wherein neurology played no part. Now art is tainted by printouts electronically calibrated, and beauty, not math and science, under-rated.

Of such criticism aren't you, as I am, sated?

70. CREATIVITY UPLIFTED

Oh, for the willfull, playful, single-minded breeze,
That picks my courage up and drops
my creativity upon the mountain tops.
Whence gazing down I spy, decry my old self's lazy ease.

Whatever shall I seek thereon to paint, compose, invent?
That might justify and validate this move on high,
And to my former incapacity and indolence give the lie?
Thereby to one and all prove my creative bent?

71. TO SEE THE WORLD AS E.E. CUMMINGS DID, (BIS)

then what is obvious must be hid; what undone be deftly did.
    else the world would be as openly revealed as *Genesis:*
not revealed at all. no, to get at old e.e. you'll have to be
    a Master of Absurdity and contra-diction, like *Genesis,*
with its occasional poetic benediction; e. e. avoided patterns,
    making total nonsense the modern choice.

does anyone have "eyes that smell of the sound of rain"
    unless they have been crying all day from thunderous pain?
His ladies' eyes were "frailer than most dreams are frail"
    but whatever those orbs did see, it was true her ears
warily beheld what those frail rain sound smelling orbs left
unheard;
    and since "frailer than most deep dreams are frail" unnoticed.

all this wouldn't matter much if "with every least each most
remembering,"
    who cared but edward estlin cummings? such "remembering"
would not
require knowing to support the world's convictions–all disputed
    by those knowers–"every least though most forgetting" one, as
e.e. said before he came undone and, "Nobody knows where
truth grows…"

to sum up, old e. e. was busily subverting so much that we as
reality–
    frail eyed–claim to see. He never to my unknowledge wrote i
think of
optometry howsoever frail our rain sound smelling eyes may be
    might we yet not all agree that what weighs heavily also
lightly does?

Barbara Sher Tinsley

to see the world as cuming didn't would be to deny as did e. e.
    a "poem huger than the grave" is permitted only
to those whose permits have expired and whose ears "my darling"
    (let's don't forget the ears) "unless we from one bird do learn
to sing"
"somewhere (you) have never travelled" i.e., the impotence
    of "diminished virility." *Vir* meant man; *virgo,* woman. Latin.

Even Romans knew as did e. e. that what seemed totally unlike's
    a kissing cousin: "girlboys and boygirls" were not news to him
who saw *vir* opened everything and *virgo* sometimes wouldn't.
    She had the most "deep throated eyes," perhaps because
they were so "frail;" borrowing from a nearby organ compensated.

In any case, the "primeval silence of her hair" prevented not
    her fingers smaller than the rain from combing it.
to see the world as cummings saw you must inherit his
    mother's "petal eyes" and thus never to have taken in at all
his face which was "a flower" and without hands made it even
harder
    not just to see e.e. but handle him. *Could* anybody handle him?

Perhaps the "keen primeval silence of your hair" let you
    "move through theys of we" which, with your great fragility
must have tired you, though you did "completely dare be
beautiful."
    Most women do not look their best when tired.
I would guess it had to be so lovely of him to see her weariness.

What with him meeting "King Christ"–in Harvard Yard?
    We do not know precisely; but what he said was that nearer him
than you he in his view (I mean e.e.'s not j.c.'s)
    was "made of nothing except loneliness." And yet, he didn't,
as I recall, offer him a doughnut and a cup of coffee;
    an opportunity to sit and chat.

72. CHOPIN'S OPUS 58: A SONATA TO MME. THE COUNTESS E. DE PERTHUIS

Some write poetry, others just send mail–
Chopin's pianistic poetry could not, unlike my writing, fail.
Poems that I write do rhyme, make music in their way–
but I would give them o'er at once if I could learn to play
Chopin's Opus no. 58. I cannot tell how a sonata,
sublime lyric, ever got to be this great. That I cannot play or
equal it in writing is quite decidedly my sad fate.

The first four notes–each one a letter–introduce
a miracle of tenderness, in B-Minor key–a melody
introduced by those four notes descending. This is the start of
paeans quite unending, to la Comtesse, E. de Perthuis.
Who was she? How did she merit thirty-seven pages of
movements sweet as claret?
And aren't we lucky, though we may not play it,
just to drink it in and share it?

The critic notes that it is crisp at first, then iridescent;
That in the key of D, turns into an *aubade*, a lover's farewell
morning greeting. But he is wrong. This is a song and it's
thematic, not fleeting.

B-major, says the critic, is emotion's sweet return, and thus,
another greeting. The ending, un-sonata like, caused Madame's
ears to burn, being, says he, a love-lyric quite exotic. We too
thrill with every trill and our ears burn in turn.

All poets and musicians could surmise, not to Madame E.'s
surprise, was that Frederick was quite caught up in the erotic.

73. E-MISSIONS OF LOVE

If I wrote you a love letter, more valuable than gold,
Would you wear it in a locket until you should grow old?
If I wrote to you a sonnet, the kind that lulls, not jars,
Could you memorize it, dear, and recite it under stars?
If I should carve my epitaph upon a marble stone
Would you emerge at gloaming, dropping roses, all alone?
But now–for electronic mail's regarded as discreet–
If I should send you, via Twitter, with 40 strokes, a tweet–
While at home I'm frying fritters, honey covered, nutty, sweet–
Would you leave your place for mine, meet me face to face to eat?
Should I then pour wine, light candles, Auntie's china on my table,
Serve you salad, sing a ballad, make you as happy as I'm able–
Hold your chair; smooth your hair, pour *café filtre* from a caraffe,
When I asked you next, could we have sex? would you acquiesce?
Or laugh?

74. ALLITERATIVE LITANY

Assorted astronomical assaults upon
economies of unconsidered, yet considerable time.
We mostly, inconsiderate, wandered wondering
through our prime–through fantasies perfumed
by thyme, raining blue florets on our fatuity–seamless
satisfactions of what seemed to us acuity.

Sweetly scented our serenity; unquestionably
obscenity sublime. Not all we noted noticed us–monotonies
did un-notified abound–while litanies of lust and listlessness
surrounded us. Anomalous, the sound of crickets creaked,
while crayfish crept unsteadily, if readily, and headily
toward the wind swept black sand beach.

Whereon gelatinous jellyfish and slimy weeds lay strewn.
The creaking cricket chorus ceased their song as swiftly
upward rose a purple moon. The creeping crayfish did not
the desolate desert of sand beach e'er reach, nor
see the sea–so eerily had earth's economies, topographies,
demographies stained and drained the seas.

We showed unceasingly our sufferance of stultifying selfishness,
and put our values' valedictory on our ease;
And stifled stupidly by selfishness all else for our ease–
Patiently with purposeful impartiality pursuing
Adventitious but ambitious adulation of our own, carefully
Home grown; such homicidal adulation of our own misdoing.

75. BOOK

My book, my life, adventure, story
begun in drabness ends in glory–
Cardboard covers, cloth, or leather
What freight it bears we bore together.

Book, when all is read and done,
'tis Thou who brought me rays of sun–
and made the darker hours flee–
Bound together, you and me.

76. ARCH

Poets, communicate. Don't be arch.
Not mischievous or saucy. Don't hide
your wisdom 'neath the larch.
Of arches to the bold we've quite enough, I say.
Trajan's, Diocletian's, Constantine's, Marble Arch.
The one down on the *Champs Elysées.*
Poets shouldn't hide under an arch.
Those commemorate soldiers; killers
on the march. A poet should be forthright,
never arch. Put starch into peoples'
lives, remembering not conquerors, but
husbands, children, wives. A poet cannot do this,
if he hides his meaning under any kind of span.
A poet should be a clarion clear, and champion
of the common, not uncommon, man.

Barbara Sher Tinsley

77. BEMUSING PERSISTENCE

Art, history, humor, science, philosophy,
lyrics, tragedy passion, more. I do not really know, at heart who
sent these tasks galore. I felt, I still feel, chosen
to receive the elements of laugher, earthiness and straw of
which Thalia thought I had sufficient store.

At any rate, I served, perhaps less well than I should
for conveyance of such varied tribute filled me with awe. I
I asked Melpomene the honor of a crown, albeit one
of laurel, a gift from Greek and thus, (consider Magna Graecia)
Italian ground. Were the Muses listening? Around?

I tried to carry out instructions to the letter. When I thought
I'd failed, I wept. I kept as best I could my powers of recall.
The world is old, and I am young, relatively speaking. And
pleasing Muses, prophets, sybils, oracles, and gods keeps one
ever in persistent thrall.

In closing, *with* persistence, let me say, I hope I may
have pleased some arbiters of poetry; the Muses most of all.

78. ALMUÑECAR SPAIN IN LATE MEDITERRANEAN SUN, A PAINTING

White zinc the sky–nearly half the canvas. Hits the sea straight
on–thin black line–
so fine the dividing line
Of Prussian blue–the sea–and titanium white–the sky.
Squared waves that in a spray of knife imposed impasto challenge
Cumulous clouds more vast, and cut them.

O Clouds of blue and white–abut them. The town,
round cone of white-limed squares bares window eyes of umber
Risen up from lower frame–a honeycomb of clay–not lumber.
So on a hot day, south of Granada, white-like flame, cleaves
roiling sea in twain after Almuñecar rises from siesta. Spanish
slumber.

79. BEACHES

Were I but sand upon the beach
and waves kept crashing within reach
of all that I identify with, being sand–
I'd shift and blow until I gained the dunes
up on the hill and built myself through
force of will a new identity. Though I could still be sand
and still be still, be as I had before the wind
and water, waves decreed that particles of
sand like me were but the slaves of ocean
peaks, ocean power, ocean will. The way to safety lay
for me not by some grim energy but by adapting to a state
of natural awe, thus limiting the wind and waves, restoring
beaches to customary reaches of a universal just and natural
shoreline law: Water, waves and winds must land;
almost invariably come to rest on sand.

80. BLUE MOUNTAIN

Blue mountain just outside my door,
anchored to my garden floor–
Must be six feet high–or more;
Covered with blue and white and striped
Morning glories.

The mountain's base? A large brown pot. Ceramic.
Raised sitting on another upside down. Dynamic.
The vines climb up on bamboo rods; the
Blooms are azure, nature's rarest hue–
A gift from all the floral gods to me, to you.

And yet, although it makes me very blue–
One day a month from now or two–
It must be taken down–its blooming through.
So many lessons from a garden may be learned.
We're born; and grow. We bloom. Are overturned.

Not just floral vines fall back from elevations-
Moses, Caesar, Lincoln, Edmund Hillary–
Whole nations. Singly and en masse we pass
From insignificance to higher status. We ascend.
Then back we fall. The patient earth awaits us. All.

81. ARCHAEOLOGICAL DIG

Years of writing, hectic pace,
Every bit of storage space in my office
filled and overflowing.

Knowing that, I fell to cleaning.
Just one cupboard drawer;
gleaming Christmas cards and more.

Shards of memory, some bright,
Archaeologist's delight. To put
it right, I sorted it all into shoeboxes.

The drawer, a midden, shiny clutter,
photographs of friends and family,
Tossed retrospectively inside.

An exhibition of a certain lack.
No volition to look so far back.
Relief not to review the past.

Yve's high school graduation flics.
A few more precious family pics.
Small mementos of a private nature.

Sweet debris of memories forgotten.
Things once precious, clear, had fled.
A lifetime of things dear, some dead.

Then, underneath still more detritis,
I uncovered what I never thought
Were there. Poems of adolescence.

Not innocence. A cache, a stash of poems
sent me in the 70s from Mom, entreated once
this stuff to "Save." For decades "lost" inside my "cave."

An archaeologist of the mind, finding such
artifacts left behind would rave. I did not rave.
I wept. Of my youth I've now recovered much.

Oddly, the twenty-some poems written as a girl,
Were on a par with those I've since composed.
Who knows? They might even be superior.

I only know they are not at all inferior.
Their style, it seems to me, is more restrained,
has meter, less rhyme; not less meaning.

I cannot say why Melpomene fled for over
half my being. But she is back with
measured thoughts, humor, rhyme, and seeing.

Barbara Sher Tinsley

82. POETRY READINGS

Why do I share my poems at a formal reading?
Why should my most casual and my private
thoughts formality be needing? Casualness is, after all,
formality's reverse. As for privacy, what but a public reading be
    worse?

There must be more to rhyming, an impulsion of the soul–
than reading it to others–not most poets' goal.
But reading it aloud to those whom it may please,
brings my spirit happiness, purpose, psychic ease.

83. WHILOM THOUGHTS

Whilom thoughts, the half-forgotten past–
batter my tired brain–like hailstones on windows,
crying "Let me in; let me have at what you cannot redo.
Your happiness, your pain. Such thoughts, a varied past,
rest in an alcove where I garner as much memory as I can.
Time changeth every living thing, and that "road not taken"
line comes back to haunt me. Not the beckonings of two
but a whole nexus of roads–taken–or not. Whilom thoughts.

Barbara Sher Tinsley

84. ART AND EXCELLENCE, A RONDEL

What cannot righted be, must be forever wrong.
Such perfection as we seek may not be taught.
The artistry that leads to it by discipline is wrought;
Art's excellence, our need of it, we praise in song.

The casual dilettante, shall not art haunt for long–
His will's too shallow, too unstable and too fraught.
What cannot righted be, must be forever wrong.
Such perfection as we seek may not be taught.

The product of an artist's hand is pure and strong.
No effort's by it spared or shared another's thought–
Nor any error rectified however long 'tis sought;
What cannot righted be must be forever wrong.

85. LE GRAND PALAIS SUR LES CHAMPS ELYSEES ET LE PONT ALEXANDRE III

Bold gold frame encasing a Parisian sky–
   Autumnal blue. Some clouds–not yet
threatening above the pleated rearmost domes.
   A tower of stacked doughnuts with a slanting
roof, looking quite aloof out toward the entrance
   on the Pont Alexandre Trois, whose own gold
decoration vies with the museum for attention,
   though it will not from the Grand Palais
get any condescension.

Across the Seine, I have my paints lain out on the
   granite parapet beside the walk. Passers-by
will stop and talk. I let them.
   I must forget them to finish before dark.
A chill wind springs up. That sky will not stay
   blue. I do take time to answer two girls from
Texas, asking, "Where is the street called *Rue*?"
   I paint the spate of Seine that fills with
every kind of boat and barge; heavy river traffic.

I've done the boats. Now, for the trees; their crowns
   of gold do me please more than when they're green.
Nearly November. Soon those leaves will fall. By December
   this show of gold will leave no glowing ember.
I quickly paint the murky cement wall. A pyramid
   is possibly a patriotic one commemorating what for me
is no known victory. Each nation vaunts its own.
   To be American in Paris one celebrates most victories alone.

That lion seems to guard a flight of steps that once descended
would let me read who or what was of a pyramid in need.
Now, for the *quadriga*, nearest the Seine: horse chariot
depicting Harmony besting Discord. Hard to guess that
   harmony is
that green horseman with hand extended to the sky.
He seems a conqueror with whom one shouldn't mettle.
In France the rule was never lightly with an enemy to settle.
So far from what I think that harmony should make its norm–
but I just paint Parisian culture. I do not her culture form.

I have done my best to paint the Grand Palais seen from the Seine.
Its front façade, with complicated colonnade, would do me in.
Besides, where out in front could I have found a place to put stuff?
And from the Champs itself, I would likely have been crushed
by all those people strolling its sidewalks, the *trottoirs*–
the boulevard itself, with its endless streaming cars.
Better to have gone as I did go to the Seine's other side, a
stream of beauty. My duty was to choose it. I had reasons:
reflections of Paris's most splendid flow of seasons.

86. THE GIRL WITH A PEARL IN HER EAR
BY VERMEER

The girl with a pearl in her ear by Vermeer turns away
from the gloom toward the light of the room–if this is a room.
There's no definition, and mere intuition is the sole condition,
making her confusion and apprehension unclear.
We're bound by illusion–so, too, was Vermeer.

He records no commotion, much emotion, some fear.
Is there any danger here? What might seem strange to her?
What enlighten her? frighten her? brighten
her prospects for today, for tonight?
We cannot say. We have no right, no insight.

The girl in her turban of crystalline blue and gold's
urban, well off, neither bold nor suburban.
Her eyes are a question in amber and white, irises flecked with
light. Melon lips parted– in hope or from fright?
Glance unsure. Creamy complexion. Dutch perfection.

One supposes she's pure. Here nothing's jaded!
Here nothing's faded. Here is youth. Where is truth?
Is purity her surety she may welcome this caller?
Has he come to her rescue, or just to enthrall her?
Her eyes show surprise; they are startled. In doubt.

Will she have to accompany him home? to go out
on a night that is dark, cold, and drear?
Are we seeing her hope or assaying her fear?
What might she see–but not we–here?
What might she be hearing behind that pearl earring?

Barbara Sher Tinsley

And why have you shown us this girl in suspension
Twixt answer and question, in so searching a light,
So late in the night? What does she see, hear,
feel, anticipate, fear?
Tell us, please, if you will–Johannes Vermeer.

87. SELF-PORTRAIT

A sensitive but non-committal pose,
Not trusting possibly the fingers of her hand
That paints her forehead, eyebrows hair and nose,
That gives her eyes the skepticism of
a gaze something close to doubt
And does it without condemning her to fear.

Her sunburned face aglow, she gardened,
Walked, pushed baby carts to play parks
Don't you know, or simply roamed the streets of
Florence, Paris, Aachen, Venice, in the sun.
And when all that was done, returned to spend
Her time in dim lit carrels in Stanford's stacks.

What could she show, what should she know about
The pitfalls, prizes of a scholar's life? She was a gardener,
seamstress, painter, cook, a hostess, and her husband's wife.
The paths she trod, through English feminism, and through
The Reformation's strange ideas of God kept her in line. And
fallen out, discovered references of a literary kind.

Barbara Sher Tinsley

88. COMING OUT TO OTHERS

I passed my day in contact with three friends.
I made a point to give them all the dividends of
my quite quiet but not uncheckered career–
in writing, prose, poetry and relationships. In what
Might pass for marriage counseling.
How different this day from those in
which I stay at home alone; tending
my garden; writing memoirs, novels, poetry–
making dinner.

89. TRANSPERSONAL RELATIONSHIPS.
A CONTEST.

The *trans* part was quite clear–to go beyond, cross over.
But really, crossing the personal seemed impersonal, giving up
    personae.
Yours and Mine. Those I deem fine. The special things that
    make me–and us–easy to define.
Could I give up my psyche thus to win a prize?

I read the contest's rules one more time. "Twenty
interpersonal poems," about the giving up or giving over,
crossing into fields–no, bogs–wherein might grow
alternatives to all behavior that we know;
A different kind of savior; masterful. Forgiving? Yes and no.

Transpersonalized means–I guess–beyond ourselves,
reaching others–other lives, states of being and perception.
Other spans of time. Timelessness a fragment of the personalized
    Other;
Fragment is a guess. Crossing of material me to spaces lacking
    matter can cause stress.

And surely every poem I write is personal transpersonalized?
In that I read it to you, and you nod, is not that prized?
The catsup label, Stop Sign, RX on my pills and most, though by
no means, all computer cookies, do they not cross over?
Do I leave no transpersonal impression on hard drive? Lover?

Are we to our friends, students, colleagues, doctors, not
transpersonal enough? Would they appreciate
us more if we went under cover with transpersonality
more sure? The subject itself suggests a cure for
what is seemingly impenetrable and obscure.

Barbara Sher Tinsley

Go, be transpersonal to the neighbors, your neighborhood.
Go, see if it will do them or me or you or us more good than
Offering a helping hand, proffer sympathy for loss;
Assure them they are as dear to you as you are to your own.
Transpersonal works when we help those who are most alone.

90. LIKE MUSIC

Poetry when it's good has meter;
music has a beat.
I like my coffee strong, my poetry and music, sweet.
And if, by chance or circumstance,
both may have meandered,
Ah, Melpomene and Euterpe,
Please keep to one sole standard:
That we, all three, may touch the hearts of all
We choose to soothe, enthrall.
And poets, let Apollo find
We have as well as heart, a mind.

91. GLADIOLI

The word derives from *gladius* (Lat.), meaning sword.
Not that I plant gladiators in my yard. Yes, their leaves come up
sword shaped, I know. But their blooms are ruffled, feminine
and make a lovely show.

Show me the warriors, the gladiators, centurions, doughboys,
Dog-faced men at arms that have our craven politicians, boys
and all reporters charmed from Herodotus to MacArthur, and I
will show you men for whom blood was but fertilizer.

I will show you men for whom rotting carcasses were as corm.
Men who denied the norms of peace and gardening
which make the heart joyous, spirit bouyant, eye glad of vision and
nose delight in perfume filling the night garden.

Gladioli. I dove into clay pots and planted them to see their
swords arise. Not to deride them, for I take pride in them.
I planted those formal, ruffled flowers on stalks that
never fight, having no business but to glorify beauty.

I plant them as a duty, to bring them by the armful
In ranks that are not harmful, but guaranteed
to dispel the slightest hint of gloom.
And make more civilized my living room.

Can soldiers dispel gloom? Their weapons are not like gladioli
shoots, who never shoot to kill or wound.
Which is why I wish the flower that I call my favorite
had a claim to a more peaceful name than gladioli.

92. TRUST

Trust is such a precious thing,
It can't be borrowed, can't be learned.
Trust makes the lover's touch a
mansion for the heart; a grotto for the mind–
and must be earned.
Trust is faith in someone caring,
encouraging, supporting, sharing; filling the
lowest depths of true love's death–
strengthening the loved one's sense of worth.
The topic least discussed that fosters love is trust.

93. KITE

Call me a kite, a simple shape–diamond,
with stakes crossed so, a tail drags behindhand.
The tail's for stability, since I ascend to the sky–
and may never be stable without it to fly.

Call me a kite, a colorful tissue.
I'm up and away, unburdened by issue.
I fly but am held by a man on the ground,
tail, male and headwinds dictate where I'll be found.

Found on the ground, despite all defiance;
pulled down by the wind, and by man in alliance.
Found on the ground is the best kites can do.
Call me a kite; give me a tail; let me ascend again into a gale.

Twisting and swirling, listing and curling; unstable, unguided,
untutored, decided. Call me a kite that is short-lived but able to
go where she listeth and twisteth. No label. Turn in the wind;
race up a mountain; richochet down–into a fountain.

Call me a kite, but don't give me stability.
Let me attest to and display my beauty, agility.

94. LAUGHTER

Why, when the world is laughing 'round me
has so little of it found me?
I write novels witty, bright, replete
With jocund thoughts and jokes–
But though I *write* them well enough,
Laughter's reserved for other folks.

Laughter is a gift contrived
for those of tragedies deprived.
Not for skeptics, or those who spent their
days in scholarship, reflection, art–
From laughter's easy panaceas
the gods have set me quite apart.

Barbara Sher Tinsley

95. STREAM OF CONSCIOUSNESS

My stream of consciousness did twist and flow
and at many a marsh and indentation of its banks
did slow–making me wonder if rivers of the mind
set memory adrift–or left it far behind? I knew that it
pursued a twisting route, had passed youthful apprehension
and adolescent angst acute; did course through
fields of butter cups and Queen Anne's lace;
set me a merry chase to keep its waters ever in my sight.
It rolled past farms and forests dim. I lost my memory of him.
It passed high walls of rock and flowed 'neath many a
mountain's crest, until its darker turns reminded me
that one who yearned for such a river seldom kept abreast–
And then this keeper of my conscious memories, my past,
eluded darkness and at last turned silver in the morning's light.
And there it dropped me in your sight. So strong the river's
long trajectory had led; and, happy in its own deep river bed,
delivered me–quite casually–to yours.

96. OUR VOYAGE OUT

Not to be calm upon life's stormy tide
is proof that one is not becalmed upon
the sea of life, which does not smoothly flow.
Its tides are strong; its undercurrents
unpredictable. Those calm upon this voyage
underestimate how deep the fathoms lie under
the deck; how swift the waters pass; how
deep the troughs of the most shallow waves.

Something may indeed be said for calmness,
but only when the voyage ends, the ship puts
into port. The passengers 'til then are well
advised until it docks to be prepared for all
that may go wrong; to man the lifeboats if any
be aboard; if they are not first lowered by
the captain's crew, leaving no space for you.

If so, and finding that you're on the deck,
take a running leap into the sea. Try to land
near something large and buoyant. Nothing is more
apt to calm one in life's sea than something
large that floats. Better, life boats; worse the mind,
which is, you'll find, no refuge; being very small and
heavy. Nothing weighs one down like calmness.

Barbara Sher Tinsley

97. VIRGINIA SUNSET IN FALL
(PHOTOGRAPHED BY CLAIRE J. TINSLEY)

Tapestry of orange watered silk, canary yellow streaked,
Late autumn sky ablaze with light.
O'er worked with bare tree limbs–white oak
poplar, silver birch, birds; all black against the sky.
A tapestry to put the Bayeux tapestry to shame;
for here is no one slain. Instead, all weary folk
may gaze in wonder and delight at this exquisite sight,
embroidered blaze of Old Dominion countryside
in fall before the fall of night.

98. GLIDING FANCY

Serpent-like among the foliage in my brain
my fancy glides, weaving, graceful, handsome.
Ubiquitous, I cannot seem to shake it off, but
through some transom carelessly left open
it slithers after me. Then, turning suddenly to face
its laughter, it withers me with such burning
coals of eyes my very soul is turned to ashes.

99. DRIED HYDRANGEAS

Hydrangeas–water loving–grow in my yard
   'til summer's end, and though they soak up moisture
greedily, turn dry as wall paper; blended hues of white.
   pink, green, blue, and as the fall sets in, brown, too.

Had you seen these blooms in spring their variegated
   palette would have caused your eyes to sing, and you'd
have sworn the hose I used had into roses them transfused.
   You'd have erred, but I've made worse mistakes.

There are worse terrors than drying out and changing color.
   We age, grow more dependent on our drink, lose beauty
and the will to think–unlike hydrangeas–who some claim do
   from aging gain. An old refrain. Its untruth causes pain.

100. PAPERWHITES

I took this morning, as my mission–
though I had no real commission,
to grasp my trowel and in demission
to fall weather, plant a hundred paperwhites–or
more–several score.

These flowers, whiter than the snow
are bloodied o'er by myth, you know.
You see Narcissus, handsome youth,
mistook his image for a nymph–in truth
inhabitants of fountains.

He cried out, if I cannot have her, no more palaver.
I shall kill myself and end it all. He did, because he could.
The gods turned his blood to narcissi and
called them good. Narcissi, harbingers of cold.
When my garden's a burned ember; so one day
in December, I'll have him to remember.

If I mitigate the dreary weather because
Narcissus knew no other way to live or love
than suicide, then fine. If I bring about false
spring in winter in anticipation–it's mine.
That's why I hid his last remains in soil; t'was worth my toil
    and hope.

I did it for his father, Cephisus,
and for his mother, Leriope.

Barbara Sher Tinsley

We bring children forth in pain and blood, a
dangerous season. For Narcissus, nature's diapason
rang so clearly. He sacrificed life for no reason.
I plant my paper whites as tokens of a kinder force
than mere self-love and admiration. Though
on reflection, we share one destination.

101. STAGED

The world's a stage
And staged so carelessly
The set unsettled
Moves the action.

Benumbed, the audience
Assumes all roles and
Stages the world to represent
The characters.

Who, with the author–
should any exist–
And actors, exit stage door
after the director.

The world then folds.
The curtain unfolds.
The management assumes
no responsibility

for your inconvenience,
nor your financial –
never mind emotional–
loss.

102. LOW HANGING FRUIT

She parked below, just where Peach Hill ran down.
Walked up the hill, a Saratoga road.
Climbed over brush into some private woods.
Descended the ravine now three years dry.

She was still young, or so I supposed.
No one here knew her, and I didn't read
Anything in the local papers about her life.
One guesses it didn't meet her expectations.

She found a tree that wasn't hard to climb.
She had prepared the rope before at home.
Delved into her backpack for its hairy loop,
And having slipped it on, she swung.

The neighbors up above did not see the body.
Perhaps she'd worn a somber shade
for such a somber task. When I reached the ravine,
I couldn't ask the police. They wouldn't talk.

But someone *was* talking. One neighbor heard a man
on her cell phone screaming something indistinct. Her name?
Unknown. He kept repeating the words "all a mistake."
The neighbor did a double-take. Phoned 911.

Low hanging fruit's the easiest to pick.
They plucked it with no trouble in no time at all
From the place where it hung drooping in the shade,
That's what kept it from rotting in the summer sun.

This crop was no doubt precious and unique,
Though its owner did not value it enough.
Perhaps she doubted its color, shape
and sweetness would sell at market price.

103. STRINGS OF PEARLS

Our lives are strings of pearls–
each day another jewel is lost.
Forget the cost. There are others.

Each one is something done
or left undone. The loss of one
means nothing in particular.

So go our lives, each with his own
strand curled, put away some place–
the oysters' comely artifice.

Here and there, sickness, care.
We had so large a share of pearls it
mostly didn't matter.

The strand didn't shatter. No.
It imperceptibly diminished, though,
as one by one it came undone.

We caught a glimpse of us at fifty-five.
Still healthy, still alive. The pearls
in all their luminosity kept falling.

Maintained the same velocity. Called to us
as each fell, do not forget. Do well. For
how long would the strand stay strong?

The pearls returned unto the sea of life and
were restrung upon the ocean's floor; then
redistributed to unborn children more.

Recycling of the pearls, you see, is really just
humanity; each pearl's a day we failed to cherish.
Each retains its glow. It is we who perish.

104. FLAUTIST. BERKELEY, '64

Once she stood on Telegraph.
Blue, white, yellow striped turban.
Strong, long hair. Denim shirt. Sandals. Jeans.
Another of your 1960s Berkeley scenes.

At her feet an old felt hat. Would you,
could you put your spare change into that?
your dollars? Was she one of U.C.'s scholars?
Her being there was Being There.

Playing "Greensleeves." That good old air.
She played as if she didn't care that you
or she or anyone she knew was there.
No calculation on her part what we'd give.

Could you give? She had to play to live.
And now she's living on my wall above the fireplace.
She plays forever at a leisured, flawless pace.
Why did I make her background so deep red?

Perhaps I felt she'd vanish against blue instead.
A flautist flouting all the rules of decorum
and mulling while she played for you if she should
phone her folks for cash?–Or seek a better forum?

Had this flautist flouted all parental rules?
Her karma, one might gather, was to play her flute
wherever–street corners, bars at dark, in daytime,
Peoples' Park. Maybe, in one of many music schools?

And now she's living on my wall above the fireplace.
Would she still recognize her turban, flute, the place?
Could she, my age nearly, still play that folksong clearly?
Has kismet given her a mature form? A time-graced face?

105. GROWTH AND HEALING BY POETRY

It's been a good year for healing, though I've not been ill.
A plethora of things didn't go well; and still it's been
annealing. It seems misfortune's turned into a sealing,
as of old when saints were sealed and given halos gold.

My losses–a job terminated–one I'd loved for over thirty
years healed–me. Strengthened my resolve to solve another
set of challenges; find new friends. Strengthened me in part;
I see that truth when dreaming, or when opening my heart.

It's been a good year for healing. I have found another voice,
Although I did not speak in tongues before; of books on history,
I'd written four and articles in journals and encyclopedia. More.
That knowledge disseminated, I feel intellectually un-freighted.

My eyes are now unveiled–an ophthalmologist
prevailed. I have clearer sight. But it's not just distance
that is clearer. No, I've come to hear as well see things dearer than
all to which I did aspire: songs from a frescoed inward choir.

106. THE LOVERS' SESTINA

I.

I ought not in these times so somber
Look for treasures of great price,
When riches have I of more worth
Than any that are mined or made
Withal. Thy sweet tenderness to me
From lips like wine, your sweet concern.

II.

How we met and woo'd–of whose concern?
I hear so many tales of matches somber.
All your promises rained sweetly down on me.
None shall be sold, no not for any price.
Nor do I cast a glance at 'spousals made
That some imply are of far more worth.

III.

Our pleasures–nay, the secrets that we share are worth
The total sum of all the world's concern.
And while the world doth spin, is it made
More bright, more beautiful by being somber?
Let those who deal in frowns now alter price
and bargains made in ignorant reproofs of me.

Barbara Sher Tinsley

IV.

All read the published bans for you and me.
And recall reading not to figure up our worth;
For nothing real like true love boasts a price.
Nor anyone who cannot see that be of great concern.
The priest who shall officiate may yet seem somber –
Until sprinkling at the font what our true love has made.

V.

Hearts are not by chance found but by reflection made
To order for their claimants. They're for you and me.
I could not, surely, be content with heartbeats somber,
Nor continue long to be enraptured by their worth.
State diplomats and couriers, have each their own concern.
But nothing they may do outdoes your kiss's price.

VI.

Now dress, guests all, without concern for price,
Now pours our finest wine from blue grapes made.
Now leave all weariness behind with fears, concern–
And all who love life and love rejoice with you and me.
Such music as by angels bowed on violins is worth
A tripping dance; skipping o'er what e'er be somber.

ENVOI

Come; and by me loving you let all exalt love's worth;
Dismiss the price that is by celebration made.
There'll be somber reckoning enow; for now of no concern.

107. FALLING LEAVES

Everything I sought to do, to bring
into fruition, give to you
had failed its mission–derailed from
what at length on you prevailed.

Perhaps my heart's the reason,
beating out of season, *it* de-railed,
and staled the gift I would have made
but for untimely beauty, leafy shade.

You who expected little from me
at the start–sat silent, but with waiting,
hopeful, private and deprivèd heart.
You thought of me a duty at the start.

That passed, our mutual admiration
was the tide on which we drifted,
until in months–not many–our feelings,
like leaves in piles had downward sifted.

And so that smile of yours that ever
remained keen, lit up the days in
academe that would have else been drear;
and took my love before another year.

Of that, I think, you never entertained a fear.

108. THE CREEK BESIDE THE NORTH PASTURE

I put an apple, cookies, trail mix and Perrier in my canvas sack,
with a book and scaled the North Pasture. The pond behind
the gray-red barn was golden; jade; weed choked; once I'd left
the gnarled chestnut, now partly leafed, partly dying, there was
no shade. All but the pond was drying. August. East Chatham
in the Berkshires.

The rutted path laid down by tractor wheels was hard and dry,
free of Queen Anne's lace, buttercups, milkweed. Until this
week I hadn't made this trek since....when? Since I was nine
or ten, and then came for wild strawberries in June, blackcaps
later on; the view. I must go see before descending if any still be
there fending off dry weather. None.

The bushes rise up with the hill and from the top of slanted land
lay half of Berkshire County, countryside; ignoring–as I did–
the Thruway. As a child I drew those Berkshire hills, with lavender
against the bowl of faded blue that covered me, acreage, barn and
farmhouse, too. I crayoned my environs on typing paper.
The child as artist.

There, where the pasture dips down into woods runs a creek,
the path is steep, and half grown over, though I carved my way
down twice this week already. Steady, braced against the steep
hillside, I wound my way slant-wise until I found myself astride
the bank. The creek, lower than when I was ten, was running still.

Upon the edge hard earth and gnarly roots of pine and birch.
To read I must shed my shoes and lurch into the stony bed
where, wading out between small boulders, find the shoulders
of a giant flat-topped stone. It is a monument to the creek;
to where I fished for bullheads when a child alone. My old
familiar stone.

I settled down to read–some Yeats, Auden, Eliot, Berry. I thought
they would all have loved this very scene of nature, mild,
not wild, but with a pioneer, an undeveloped mien. When lost in
not light reading, I suddenly became aware of twigs snapped
clean–the sound of pebbles, hard earth, showering down
ground receding.

Turning, I saw, descending my own private path–the only one
around–a sunburned face, an out-back hat, a man with easel,
staff, blue jeans and backpack. Move out? I wouldn't
have fled an artist. "Hello," he said, "My name is John, and I am
here to paint the stream. May I?"
My paradise, my Uncle's land. What say I? "Yes, you may."

He set up on the shore, and I stayed on the rock. Dappled
sunbeams on my face, my book. I read. "Don't look up, don't
need you to pose," this artist of the wilds would have me to
suppose. Fine by me. I gave myself to Yeats. He'd entered
through so many female gates. An hour passed. That stone
grew hard.

John announced, "It's done. Some fixative and it's good
to go. Come see." I did, then I resumed my stony place
not yet alone. John was there a while, watching me.
In chalk, ink, watercolors he revealed my face. Portrait severe.
He didn't get from me a smile. He maintained good cheer.
John preferred to keep it: "For I see you won't be happy hanging it.

Rather than slip it into a drawer, I pledge to do another,
where your elegance comes to the fore. When may I have the
chance?"
He looked at me, and shifted burdens. Smiling. I saw what I'd
not seen before. He was beguiling.

The last of Indian summer, too, right through October, John drove
to the farm and kept me company; no, we kept company.
He was to have an art show in Stockbridge. At his studio.
He'd park near the barn and draw me in the garden, my office,
at the pond. He said not looking up, "Of you I'm growing
fond."

Fall ended and the weather changed. The red and gold leaves fell.
Tourists disappeared when "leafing" lost its spell. John drove up
one day early in November. He brought three unsold portraits
of me, saying: "I started painting you because you did not
smile. I wonder if I marry you, you will, once in a while?"
I said, "It's worth a trial."

The creek below the North Pasture became our sacred place.
It was John and only he who put a smile upon my face.

109. SENTIMENT

A sentiment's a feeling written in the mind,
the breast, the heart's own diary.
Sentiment is never blind to what's expected
of it when you needs must part.
It lingers lovingly when you are far away.
It wiles away the hours 'til the day
When your return to all you love is imminent,
And when it is, you will find sentiment.
Returned to your familiar haunts and places,
Reunited with the dearest of all faces, your lover's–
your mate's–and having met your every distant goal,
you'll find that sentiment is keeper of the soul.

110. DESIRES OF A SEA CAPTAIN'S WIFE

Of all the many things of yours I am,
one is the sandy beach on which you land
after a voyage lasting a long eight months–
in which as you now know your son was born.
I am the link that makes your name live on.

I want to be the hearth that keeps off cold,
and in your absence did invest the gold
you left to keep our household safe from harm–
which by wise investing I have tripled.
I want to be the grog on which you tippled.

I want to be more than our son's mother.
I want to be more than just your lover.
your benefactress and chamberlain–
the varnished deck you stand on in the rain;
the wind that fills your top sail, sways your mast.

I want to be your present and your past–
the wooden planks that form your very boat;
the sea upon which you and your crew float.
I want to be the profits that you make;
the one who lies beside you when you wake.

I want to be the wake that churns behind your stern.
I want to be the port for which you yearn.
I want to be the anchor that you drop
The number on the pier at which you stop.
Whatever's right for thee, I want to be.

111. LOVE'S CORE

Hope that is the core of love–
hope that longs to soar above
the hopelessness of daily trials–
hope that overcomes the tears, now smiles.
We're tempted by so many hoped for things,
that's true. But what I hoped for most and got–
and still have in my heart is you.

112. BLUE ROOM ORANGE CHAIR, TWO WOMEN?

Was it the fascination of bareness in this blue room with
orange chair that kept one woman staring at the corner,
disconsolate, as rectilinear as her oh so straight back?

The fact that she was perched upon the chair's one arm
made her intense inattention to her friend
all the more arresting.

And why was the friend an S-shaped curve, head down on chair,
in formal gown, draped over blue carpet,
so deeply sleeping?

All the two had in common was their detachment from each
other. Or else they were the same woman in two different
costumes? Moods? Times? Contemplating the possibilities of
love in art? in life?
Only the chair knew.

113. A PLACE AT THE TABLE

I don't write poetry like Yeats.
I can't compete with e.e.c.
Their lyricism and libido were too great;
I am constrained to write like me.
I will avoid all themes historical
like T.S. Eliot's, adept of the allegorical.
Those nimble witted master bards
Could reduce my utterance to shards.
Yet, striving still for something worth the lines of
those now one with earth, I set aside all private dearth of art.
I play my own unique if lesser part as well as I am able;
Hoping to find a seat at the foot of their exalted table.

FINIS

CPSIA information can be obtained at www.ICGtesting.com
Printed in the USA
LVOW12*1615040216

473713LV00002B/5/P